THE W

Wise woman

OTHER BOOKS BY RED HAWK

Journey of the Medicine Man (August House, 1983)

The Sioux Dog Dance (Cleveland State University, 1991)

Raven's Paradise (Bright Hill Press, 2010)

WITH HOHM PRESS:

The Way of Power (1996)

The Art of Dying (1999)

Wreckage with a Beating Heart (2005)

Self Observation ~ The Awakening of Conscience
An Owner's Manual (2009)

Mother Guru
Savitri Love Poems (2014)

Self Remembering
The Path to Non-Judgmental Love, A Practitioner's Manual
(2015)

Return to the Mother
*Poems of Self Remembering and Self Observation Inspired
by Lao Tsu's Tao Te Ching* (2017)

THE WAY OF THE
Wise Woman

POEMS BY
RED HAWK

HOHM PRESS
Chino Valley, Arizona

Cover Design: Becky Fulker, Kubera Book Design, Prescott, Arizona

Cover Image: Meinrad Craighead, "Wisdom." Crow Mother and the Dog God. San Francisco: Pomegranate, 2003. Used with permission

Interior Design and Layout: Becky Fulker, Kubera Book Design, Prescott, Arizona

Library of Congress Cataloging-in-Publication Data

Names: Red Hawk, author.
Title: The way of the wise woman / poems by Red Hawk.
Description: Chino Valley, Arizona : Hohm Press, [2019]
Identifiers: LCCN 2019013209 | ISBN 9781942493471 (trade pbk. : alk. paper)
Classification: LCC PS3568.E295 A6 2019 | DDC 811/.54--dc23
LC record available at https://lccn.loc.gov/2019013209

ISBN: 978-1-942493-47-1

Hohm Press
P.O. Box 4410
Chino Valley, AZ 86323
800-381-2700
http://www.hohmpress.com

This book was printed in the U.S.A. on recycled, acid-free paper using soy ink.

For Yogi Ramsuratkumar, the Wisest of Women
& the perfect embodiment of the Feminine Goddess,
His perfect Companion Ma Devaki, the Goddess incarnate,
and for His Son, in whom the Feminine flowered.

For Chandrika, the most Beloved Feminine Goddess
and for Little Wind & Rain Drop who awakened the
first stirrings of the Feminine within.

All praise be yours Beloved Goddess.

CONTENTS

i. The Wise Woman is happy for no particular reason 3

ii. The Wise Woman's vigilance is never idle 4

iii. What the Wise Woman feels, she feels with all her heart 5

iv. The Wise Woman does not cling to offense 6

v. The Wise Woman sees only Goodness everywhere 7

vi. The Wise Woman lives only from Intuition and feeling 8

vii. The Wise Woman is without fear 9

viii. The Wise Woman is a manifestation of Supreme Beauty 10

ix. The Wise Woman is wise as a serpent, gentle as a lamb 11

x. The Wise Woman lives in, and is, a mystery 12

xi. The Wise Woman is without false modesty 13

xii. The Wise Woman does not tell lies 14

xiii. Like all Humans, the Wise Woman must suffer a broken heart 15

xiv. The Wise Woman has unseen protection 16

xv. The Wise Woman is born with a radiance 17

xvi. The Wise Woman is born from the Sacred Heart of Mercy 18

xvii. For the Wise Woman the Earth is a living miracle 19

xviii. The Wise Woman is a Soul perfectly aligned   20

xix.   The Wise Woman is content with what she gets   21

xx.   For the Wise Woman, the winds of madness blow no ill   22

xxi.   The Wise Woman is one acquainted with grief   23

xxii.   The Wise Woman finds her refuge within   24

xxiii.   The Wise Woman guards her home against thieves   25

xxiv.   The Wise Woman follows the path of doubt   26

xxv.   The Wise Woman, doing nothing, achieves great things   27

xxvi.   The Wise Woman minds her tongue   28

xxvii.   The Wise Woman practices humility and restraint   29

xxviii.   The Wise Woman trusts in the unknown   30

xxix.   The Wise Woman tends her own garden   31

xxx.   The Wise Woman tends to the growth of her Soul   32

xxxi.   The Wise Woman's hands are folded in repose   33

xxxii.   The Wise Woman is grateful for the gift of death   34

xxxiii.   For the Wise Woman, everything is food   35

xxxiv.   For the Wise Woman the present is Divine   36

xxxv.   The Wise Woman learns the hard way   37

xxxvi.   For the Wise Woman forgiveness is her highest duty   38 xxxvii. The Wise Woman moves through levels of inner work   39

xxxviii. For the Wise Woman the only marriage   40

xxxix. The Wise Woman is given to outrageous laughter   41

xl. The Wise Woman knows/that only good will come of this   42

xli. The Wise Woman knows where the Divine Mother resides   43

xlii. The Wise Woman knows that Wisdom is given   44

xliii. The Wise Woman is quick to apologize   45

xliv. For the Wise Woman, if everything is food   46

xlv. The Wise Woman sees the perfection   47

xlvi. For the Wise Woman, desire/is the cause of all suffering   48

xlvii. The Wise Woman knows the power of thought   49

xlviii. For the Wise Woman, if kindness doesn't work   50

xlix. The Wise Woman learns that violence   51

l. The Wise Woman trusts old love knows best*   52

li. The Wise Woman sees that the greatest courage**   53

lii. The Wise Woman intuits when to stop eating   54

*Note: This poem appeared in different form in *Wreckage with a Beating Heart.*
**This poem, in different form, was a finalist in the *Rattle* Poetry Prize and was published in *Rattle.*

liii.   The Wise Woman seeks within   55

liv.   The Wise Woman is impartial   56

Epilogue: Buddha's 4 Noble Truths

lv.   The Wise Woman knows there is suffering   59

lvi.   The Wise Woman knows there is a cause/of suffering   60

lvii.   The Wise Woman knows there is an end/to suffering   61

lviii.   The Wise Woman knows there is a well-worn/path to that end   62

Other Titles of Interest from Hohm Press   63

Contact Information   70

About the Author   70

About Hohm Press   70

Poems

i.

The Wise Woman is happy for no particular reason
because her reason is in the flesh,
in the stone, the dirt, the Moon and the day;
it has not been stolen by the mind
so she may dance and sing and play
and never look behind
at shadows, nor ahead at the treason
of tomorrow; her mind is fresh,
unencumbered by belief so she is kind,
believes only in the changing seasons.

ii.

The Wise Woman's vigilance is never idle
and bows before no dogma or idol,
worships no plan or man, longs for no result,
is moved by the moment, what is felt
in the wind, the way a leaf throws itself
upon the mercy of every vagrant breeze;
when, in exultant joy, she goes to her knees,
it is to worship the grass, the dirt and the trees;
then she is Still, unmoving; the hurt
which Humans do has not soiled her heart.

iii.

What the Wise Woman feels, she feels with all her heart
because she is not scattered in her various parts,
but is whole and lives solely in the present moment
so she is not subject to the torment
of the past,
her grieving does not last,
she does not succumb to the sorrow
of living for tomorrow;
she hurls herself into life's raging torrent
and abandons herself to its current.

iv.

The Wise Woman does not cling to offense,
it does not matter how dire or intense
the wrong, she is quick to forgive.
She endures life's blows and hardships
and still the passion burns in her to live;
no complaint ever escapes her lips.
Against love she offers no defense,
abandons all reason and common sense
and allows her heart to be ripped and torn;
her Innocence dies each moment, the next is reborn.

v.

The Wise Woman sees only Goodness everywhere;
even the worst among us are not spared
her mercy, the content of her heart is bared,
and kindness pours forth like a spring
uncovered in a storm.
She comes into the Human world to bring
a softness to their hearts and to perform
the miracle of drawing blood from stone.
For the sins of Humans, her Goodness will atone;
her alchemy brings forth joy from despair.

vi.

The Wise Woman lives only from Intuition and feeling
while those around her are taught lying and concealing
what their hearts are intent upon revealing;
she shines with life while they live in recoil from the heart
and fear the sting and sorrow of death
because they are divided, live apart
from their feelings, while she is in love with her breath
and body; she is real and they are nothing but a thought,
divorced from the present moment and fraught
with tensions, an open wound never healing.

vii.

The Wise Woman is without fear
because she is not separate from the Source
of all life which manifests in her as love;
she is a pure, unobstructed manifestation of the Force
which sustains her joy and descends from Above,
so she is fearless; love is always near,
thus she lives in the world of the unknown,
a different dimension from those who have grown
accustomed to fear as a normal part
of their lives, entirely divorced from the heart.

viii.

The Wise Woman is a manifestation of Supreme Beauty,
therefore she sees Beauty everywhere
and in everything, is full of mercy, takes pity
on even the smallest creatures, may adore
the ant and the firefly, the stone and leaf
alike; when one of these is hurt, her grief
is another kind of Beauty; she will not be consoled
so when, by some well-meaning person she is told
that it is only a bug, she looks at them in disbelief,
the way a virtuous woman regards a thief.

ix.

The Wise Woman is wise as a serpent, gentle as a lamb
because she is not fooled by guile or sham,
looks neither compel nor deceive her,
and even the shyest of creatures believe her
to be without harm,
thus she does not cause alarm
when she draws near;
they suffer her caress without fear,
but she withdraws at once from those who are cruel.
Trusting her heart completely, she is no fool.

x.

The Wise Woman lives in, and is, a mystery
because she is not ruled by her personal history,
has no interest in what is past,
is animated only by that which lasts
beyond death and is the Source of all life,
which is love. Though her life be brief
it is not marked by scorn or strife
and when she is moved to grief
it is not colored with sentiment or belief,
but reveals the arc of love's trajectory.

xi.

The Wise Woman is without false modesty,
therefore is not compelled to cover
her nakedness because she is a lover
of the life of the body, embodies honesty
of feeling and knows no shame,
though she has real, organic Humility
which is not the result of blame
or judgment, does not arise from the futility
of trying desperately to please,
but is like one who prays on bended knees.

xii.

The Wise Woman does not tell lies
because she does not fear the truth
no matter how bad she looks in the eyes
of others; She is willing to endure their wrath
in order to preserve her native dignity,
honor her organic nobility,
and not compromise
her integrity,
which is born from a sense of self worth
inherent in her before birth.

xiii.

Like all Humans, the Wise Woman must suffer a broken heart
in order to lose her native Innocence devoid of experience
which was not paid for but was given
by grace alone, so she must fall from that heaven
of childhood into the sorrow and disgrace
of mammal desire; from this darkness she will start
on the long path to pay for a wise Innocence
born of experience, recover the organic intelligence
of the body, know her rightful place
on the Earth, and reclaim her original face.

xiv.

The Wise Woman has unseen protection,
a Source of help and undying affection
which both arises from the Mother Earth
and descends from Above,
so that it is with her before birth
and manifests in her as non-judgmental love.
She sees and accepts that the gift of death
is everywhere around her so that each breath
is a precious gift and teaches her to only live
here, now, slow to judge, quick to forgive.

XV.

The Wise Woman is born with a radiance
which either blinds or opens people's eyes
so some grow gentle and drop all defense
against love, are transparent, without disguise,
while others cannot bear to look
into the mirror love presents, are shook
to their root by looking love in its face
and are maddened by their own disgrace.
That radiance is like a light from safe harbor
which guides storm-tossed sailors to shore.

xvi.

The Wise Woman is born from the Sacred Heart of Mercy
as love, which in the mammal Human world is heresy
and is met with resistance and unbridled fear,
but love is her basic nature and so she adheres
to it in the face of overwhelming disbelief
and refusal of Humans to see what is right before them;
she pierces their hearts and comes to grief
because she can do none other than adore them.
Rather than embrace a love which would restore them,
Humans punish her like a common thief.

xvii.

For the Wise Woman the Earth is a living miracle
and every tree, stone and creature is an oracle
of infinite Wisdom and a Source of tender care;
she bonds with the Earth as with her Mother;
the Mother's love and guidance are in the very air
she breathes, her flesh is wedded to the dirt,
and when her heart is wounded there is no other
who can offer her greater comfort for the hurt.
The Earth teaches her what it is to be Female,
to freely give and serve, sensitive to the smallest detail.

xviii.

The Wise Woman is a Soul perfectly aligned
with her mammal body, so the thinking mind
is in subservience to her heart;
her body is in perfect balance, each part
doing its allotted function, none stealing
from the other, so her heart is a Source of healing
for those unbalanced in mind and emotion.
People are drawn to her heart as a moth to fire
where they are overwhelmed with Devotion,
for such harmony consumes every desire.

xix.

The Wise Woman is content with what she gets
so she is without the sorrow of desire,
accepts what is given without regrets,
makes no demand and does not require
external validation for her self worth
because she has restored what was given at birth,
an undying love and a burning inner fire
to remain plain and simple, have no debts
because she gives without making demands,
owns only what she can hold in 2 hands,
loves and dies in total Devotion to the Mother Earth.

xx.

For the Wise Woman, the winds of madness blow no ill
because there is no war within her, she does not seek to kill
or wound her opponents, only to serve and heal,
to lend a hand to those who stumble and fall,
and to love equally the emperor and the fool,
the gentle, the harsh, the mad and the cruel.
There is no human for whom she does not feel
compassion and sorrow in equal measure, all
are deserving of love and she will not fail
to give it because she bows before a greater Will.

xxi.

The Wise Woman is one acquainted with grief
because she knows life is fragile and brief
and will steal those she loves like a thief
in the dark, leaving behind a sorrow with no relief.
Life is as delicate and uncertain as a leaf
blown in the wind and no doctrine or system of belief
eases the longing for the loved one who has died;
she accepts death as part of love, but will not be denied
her mourning; love brings the full range of joy and heartache.
It is a covenant which even death cannot break.

xxii.

The Wise Woman finds her refuge within;
she does not dream of a savior
who will rescue her from sin,
but takes responsibility for her behavior,
and works within herself to atone.
Still, she does not work alone
but with others who, like her, begin
the long slow relentless labor
to sail the stormy seas of the unknown
until she reaches the still, calm inner harbor.

xxiii.

The Wise Woman guards her home against thieves;
she is as vigilant as a sentry in enemy territory,
watchful for each negative thought or emotion, leaves
nothing unobserved; unguarded thoughts are the repository
of fear and that is the greatest thief; it deceives
us into believing we are helpless, so she is wary
of thoughts which are married
to emotion; they lie and steal her equanimity. She believes
only in the present, the Source of grace, and never grieves
for the past, is not the victim of her personal history.

xxiv.

The Wise Woman follows the path of doubt,
believing nothing until she has tested it out
for herself, verified it by touching the wound
and only then is faith born in her, attuned
to what is, not what others may say.
Hers is the experiential way,
direct personal experience teaching her about
the world as it is, not theories, not what's assumed
to be true, but what her eyes have shown.
She alone makes truth her own.

XXV.

The Wise Woman, doing nothing, achieves great things
because she forces no action, accepts what life brings
and creates out of nothing
beauty, harmony, grace, just as the birds sing
for no reason save they are alive.
She does not desire or strive
for greatness, she tends to what lies before her,
gives it her full Attention, and others adore her
work because it is elegantly simple and plain.
She acts on faith alone, seeks no personal gain.

xxvi.

The Wise Woman minds her tongue;
she knows that on careless words our fate is hung
and once spoken, the harm can't be undone
but falls on barren ground like toxic dung
from which no fair fruit has ever sprung.
She quietly waits for a word fitly spoken
and until that arises, her silence is unbroken;
she grows in strength because she is reticent,
and others listen to one who is hesitant
to speak, like a clear bell seldom rung.

xxvii.

The Wise Woman practices humility and restraint,
does not lend herself to complaint,
and does not judge the affairs
of others because she knows she is no saint
but has the same flaws as her neighbor.
She does not boast or flaunt her behavior
nor does she wait for rescue by a savior,
but works for the good of all, repairs
what she breaks
and makes amends for her mistakes.

xxviii.

The Wise Woman trusts in the unknown,
that which cannot be named, because It has shown
Its Presence by Its effect on all living things:
at the exact right moment the hidden bird sings,
or longing for loved ones the phone rings
and it is them, so she knows she is never alone.
The Presence gently urges her to atone
for her missteps and in Its mercy It brings
her forgiveness, so she does for others as it is done
for her and for all things under the Sun.

xxix.

The Wise Woman tends her own garden,
works her soil, carries her own burden
and composts it, does not blame the weather
if her crop fails; whatever blooms, she is tender
in her care, lets neither weed nor pest offend her,
and is grateful to work in rain and thunder,
plants before it freezes and harvests under
hot Sun; harsh conditions do not hinder
her honest careful labor
and she gladly shares its fruits with her neighbor.

XXX.

The Wise Woman tends to the growth of her Soul
the way a good farmer cares for the soil;
forgiving those who wrong her will not fail
to feed her Soul, even when the mind screams foul
and resists such sacrifice. When she feels
she has wronged another, to quickly apologize
strengthens the Soul and helps It grow wise;
by refusing to gossip, blame, or criticize
and practicing loving kindness even with fools,
ego dies, so from its ashes the Soul may arise.

xxxi.

The Wise Woman's hands are folded in repose;
there is an unadorned elegance to her clothes,
an absence of desire in her posture and her pose;
she shows no fear of being exposed;
the stillness of her eyes, their steady gaze,
haunts because she is so inwardly composed.
Her subtle smile reveals a self control
which contains all that she feels in her Soul
and transforms it into outer grace.
She owns her face; she knows her place.

xxxii.

The Wise Woman is grateful for the gift of death
because it makes everything she touches Holy,
she worships God in every breath,
it makes the smallest complaint folly,
and gives great urgency to being kind.
She keeps her death always in her mind
so holding onto anger seems childish, a lie
which fools indulge as if they will not die.
Death makes a joy of her conscious labor
to love herself as she loves her neighbor.

xxxiii.

For the Wise Woman, everything is food
to feed her Soul, from the steady streams
of thought to the rush of emotion;
the Soul feeds on energy transformation,
negative energy into love. Not fooled by the dreams
desire spins, the Wise Woman stays steady in her attitude
and is not ruled by every changing mood.
To grow and mature, the Soul must be fed well:
just as the chick eats the yolk to escape its shell,
the Soul consumes negativity to escape from hell.

xxxiv.

For the Wise Woman the present is Divine,
the Source of all love, the heavenly gate
and the Mother of creation.
Thus, her Attention is on bodily sensation
so she avoids the trap of identification
with thoughts and the dreams of imagination.
The Soul's deepest urge is to relate
to the Source of love, so she aligns
herself with the present because her fate
depends upon a quiet inner state of adoration.

XXXV.

The Wise Woman learns the hard way,
from her own experience, that fear separates
and divides while love unites. To stay
aligned with love, she tolerates
no division within;
separation from the Source of love
is the only sin,
thus she remains open to what is Above
her in scale
so in every inner battle, love will prevail.

XXXVI.

For the Wise Woman forgiveness is her highest duty;
in its absence, love cannot survive
and her life is robbed of its inherent beauty.
She does not want to keep revenge alive
so she prays for help to forgive, both others
and their faults, and herself for the harm
which she has done to her brothers.
Any deviation from love is cause for alarm,
and brings her at once to her knees,
begging the Source of love to hear her pleas.

xxxvii.

The Wise Woman moves through levels of inner work,
beginning with self only,
the ego-driven survival strategy, the knee-jerk
selfish response to others which makes life lonely;
slowly she grows to include self and others,
recognizing that all people are sisters and brothers;
a lifetime of struggle brings about the great inner shift,
in which she places others first, which is the gift
of love's devotion; at last she merges with the Divine Mother
for whom there is no self, only others.

xxxviii.

For the Wise Woman the only marriage
is the wedding of Masculine and Feminine inside;
she works to balance these 2 inner forces
so the Divine Feminine rules with gentle hand
and the Divine Masculine serves; she understands
that to live otherwise places the carriage
before the horses;
the duty of the Masculine is to create inner sanctuary,
a safe place for the Feminine to emerge as the bride
of the Holy Union, so these 2 may marry.

xxxix.

The Wise Woman is given to outrageous laughter
because she sees she is the Divine joke,
which she took most seriously until after
she had long suffered her seriousness, and awoke
to the perfection of all things
exactly as they are. Now she sings
in the streets and is considered quite mad
by those imprisoned in their serious side.
They do not get the joke which makes her glad
to be alive; she could not be sad if she tried.

xl.

The Wise Woman knows
that only good will come of this,
no matter what this may be;
all of her life experience shows
her the perfection of what is,
exactly as it is, here and now;
nothing could be different, otherwise how
could things have worked out so perfectly?
So she is unreasonably happy,
as if every breath were God's loving kiss.

xli.

The Wise Woman knows where the Divine Mother resides,
and she labors always to dwell in Her abode;
she knows the present, here-now, is where the Mother hides
in plain sight for all to be nurtured in the Mother Lode
of Divine love, that golden treasure
for which there is no name or measure;
it is before time and occupies all space.
All Humans may seek comfort in Her embrace
unless they make the mind their dwelling place;
in that lost world, the Mother leaves no trace.

xlii.

The Wise Woman knows that Wisdom is given
not from her but from Its Source in heaven,
thus all may have access to It if they remain
in the present, the Now-of-the-body, not the brain
but the Earthly sensation which is the body's domain.
The fool thinks he alone is wise
and believes the harder he tries
to gain Wisdom, the smarter he will appear.
The Wise Woman knows Wisdom is always near
if she remains humble, clear and free of fear.

xliii.

The Wise Woman is quick to apologize
for any wrong she may have done
in order to restore relationship.
She knows
this is how Conscience grows;
just as a compass restores a ship
to its proper course, Conscience is the one
way she has to know and actualize
the Will of God, the messenger from Above
which sets her always on the path of love.

xliv.

For the Wise Woman, if everything is food
for the Soul, then all that happens is good
and she is freed from judging wrong and right,
freed from worry and sorrow.
Like a good farmer, she plows a straight
and steady furrow
between yesterday and tomorrow,
always feeding Conscience, whose Insight
keeps her on a straight and narrow
path; it maintains a loving, peaceful mood.

xlv.

The Wise Woman sees the perfection
in everything, exactly as it is here and now,
thus judgment has no attraction
for her, she is not concerned with how
things might be different. Her only reaction
is to love things as they are. She comes to know
the self as a contraction
caused by fear, a rejection
of love. Her only Law is, As Above, so below,
and her only desire is to follow.

xlvi.

For the Wise Woman, desire
is the cause of all suffering, the source
of all harm.
She seeks within herself something higher
than the mammal urges whose force
has such attraction, such charm,
and makes of the self a cheat and a liar.
Through suffering she learns that fear
is the root of desire, the urge to alter
the perfection of the way things are.

xlvii.

The Wise Woman knows the power of thought,
that it may wound and even kill,
that every battle which was ever fought
began with a thought. She keeps her mind still
so that she may know the heart's will
and allow mind to serve, not rule.
Otherwise, she remains a fool,
blown this way and that by the mind
always changing course; she is not caught
in its shifting currents, stays focused on being kind.

xlviii.

For the Wise Woman, if kindness doesn't work
she tries more kindness,*
which to the mind is madness,
a course of action it cannot comprehend,
behind which certain danger lurks.
It is this mindless
fear which creates the blindness
whose demand is always to defend,
and violence is its inevitable end.
Thus, she chooses kindness, to lend a helping hand.

*(Chogyam Trungpa Rinpoche)

xlix.

The Wise Woman learns that violence
only leads to more violence, whether by deed
or word. Thus, she cultivates silence
and speaks only when there is a need
which is greater than keeping still.
She knows that even words can kill,
but the wildest creature is tamed by gentle hand
and even the mad can understand
and respond to a word softly spoken;
loving kindness heals the heart which is broken.

𝒞.*

The Wise Woman trusts old love knows best
upon which bed to lay its fate to rest;
it is not hurried by the changing seasons
nor rushed, though mind gives a hundred reasons.
By patience and by kindness she is known;
her root goes deep, beyond the flesh and bone.
Her love flows free, not bound by time or space;
it alone escapes Death's cold embrace.
Death has no hold on her, no sway;
Death rules the dust; old love does not decay.

*Note: This poem appeared in different form in *Wreckage with a Beating Heart.*

ii.**

The Wise Woman sees that the greatest courage
isn't needed for war
but for ordinary people facing the ravage
of old age; like soldiers, they are never far
from death. When one by one
the body's systems fail, she must be brave
and face annihilation of the flesh and bone,
her Soul clinging, like a shipwrecked sailor, to love;
finally, love is all she is given
to navigate between exhaustion and heaven.

**This poem, in different form, was a finalist in the *Rattle* Poetry
Prize and was published in *Rattle*.

lii.

The Wise Woman intuits when to stop eating
and begin to do her dying;
just as the body knows when to stop breathing,
she feels when it's time to stop trying
to stay alive and lay the body down,
when the Lord of Death comes to town.
She does not rely on thinking,
it is obvious when to stop drinking;
it is a kind of prayer, laying the body down
to honor the Lord of Death coming to town.

liii.

The Wise Woman seeks within
herself that which has always been
and never changes.
Oceans may come and go, mountain ranges
rise and fall, but the Being
at the heart of the world remains,
all knowing and all seeing.
She stills her impulses, restrains
her mammal urges; it is Vigilance she keeps,
like one who watches and never sleeps.

liv.

The Wise Woman is impartial
which means she does not choose sides,
but in every decision great or small
it is the Will of God which decides;
her course is the act
of Conscience alone, in which that Will resides.
Once she is clear, she does not react
based on the heat of emotion
or on cold logic, but from her devotion
to the Will of God, both Objective and exact.

EPILOGUE:

Buddha's
4 Noble Truths

lv.

The Wise Woman knows there is suffering, everyone lives
in a hell of her own devising and there seems to be no end
to it because the mammal mind simply repeats
and repeats its stored memories until we die.
This endless suffering is the great Human lie
and, like a thief with loaded dice, it cheats
us of our natural bliss, thrice betrays our greatest Friend.
Despite this, the Wise Woman loves
moment to moment, with the intensity of her sorrow;
the immensity of her death makes a fool of tomorrow.

lvi.

The Wise Woman knows there is a cause
of suffering and it is rooted in desire,
the wish to change the course
of things as they are,
wanting what she does not have
and refusing to accept what she is given
by life; desire never believes that love
is enough, but the Wise Woman knows heaven
is the present moment, here-now, just this,
and to live in the moment is the only bliss.

lvii.

The Wise Woman knows there is an end
to suffering, which is to remain still
inside when the mind sits as the hurt
judge of all wounded beings;
her inner Stillness brings
an end to the harsh, shrill
noise of constant judgment, begins to mend
the broken pieces of the heart.
She picks up her own Cross and carries it,
lays to rest her personal history and buries it.

lviii.

The Wise Woman knows there is a well-worn
path to that end and all maps lead there,
to that inner devastation, the war-torn
Human heart, the place where
Attention dwells;
the path out of hell
passes through the broken heart
so that's where all healing has to start.
It is by loving Attention to the broken pieces
that Human suffering eventually ceases.

Other HOHM PRESS Titles by Red Hawk

THE WAY OF POWER
by Red Hawk

"This is such a strong book. Red Hawk is like Whitman: he says what he sees..." —the late William Packard, editor, *New York Quarterly*.

"Red Hawk is a true poet whose work has strong, credible feelings and excellent timing." —Richard Wilbur, U.S. Poet Laureate and Pulitzer Prize winner.

"This collection continually surprises with insights that sometimes stop the breath." —Miller Williams, winner of 1995 Academy Award of the Academy of American Poets.

Paper, 96 pages, $10   ISBN: 978-0-934252-64-5

• • •

THE ART OF DYING
by Red Hawk

Red Hawk's poetry cuts close to the bone whether he is telling humorous tales or indicting the status-quo throughout the culture. Touching upon themes of life and death, power, devotion and adoration, these ninety new poems reveal the poet's deep concern for all of life, and particularly for the needs of women, children and the earth.

"An eye-opener; spiritual, native, populist. Red Hawk's is a powerful, wise, and down-home voice."—Gary Snyder

Paper, 132 pages, $12   ISBN: 978-0-934252-93-5

To Order: 800-381-2700
Or, visit our website at www.hohmpress.com

Other HOHM PRESS Titles by Red Hawk

WRECKAGE WITH A BEATING HEART
by Red Hawk

"Red Hawk's work puts us all in the line-up...We're all guilty, and Red Hawk himself is standing next to us."—Hayden Carruth, winner of the National Book Award, 1996.

This collection of over 250 new poems is Red Hawk's magnum opus, revealing the enormous range of his abilities in both free verse and sonnet forms. Red Hawk views the world with compassion tinged by outrage. He speaks with eloquence and raw power about all that he sees, including sex, death, hypocrisy and war as well as his own failures, and his life-altering remorse of conscience.

Paper, 300 pages, $16.95   ISBN: 978-1-890772-50-5

• • •

MOTHER GURU
Savitri Love Poems
by Red Hawk

A collection of refined devotional poetry in the tradition of Hafiz and Rumi—whose poems of love continue to inspire millions throughout the world. The fact that this poetry appears in contemporary dress is more gracious still. These are poems of a truly broken heart—pleading poems, begging poems, prayers and curses, bawdy, ironic, hilarious, tough-minded, sometimes angry, often just broken. Few books of poetry today attempt to traverse this razor's edge. Fewer still can do so with respect, dignity and passion.

Paper, 208 pages, $19.95   ISBN: 978-1-935387-84-8

To Order: 800-381-2700
Or, visit our website at www.hohmpress.com

Other HOHM PRESS Titles by Red Hawk

SELF OBSERVATION ~ THE AWAKENING OF CONSCIENCE
An Owner's Manual
by Red Hawk

This book is an in-depth examination of the much-needed process of "self" study known as self observation. It offers the most direct, non-pharmaceutical means of healing the attention dysfunction which plagues contemporary culture. Self observation, the author asserts, is the most ancient, scientific, and proven means to develop conscience, this crucial inner guide to awakening and a moral life.

This book is for the lay-reader, both the beginner and the advanced student of self observation. No other book on the market examines this practice in such detail. There are hundreds of books on self-help and meditation, but almost none on self-study via self observation, and none with the depth of analysis, wealth of explication, and richness of experience that this book offers.

Paper, 160 pages, $14.95   ISBN: 978-1-890772-92-5

• • •

SELF REMEMBERING
The Path to Non-Judgmental Love
by Red Hawk

This companion piece to the author's previous book *Self Observation* offers detailed practical guidelines that allow one to know *with certainty* when one is Present and Awake. It details the objective feedback mechanisms available to everyone for attaining this certainty: Am I awake *now*? How do I know? Sincere readers will find invaluable help in answering these two questions.

Paper, 258 pages, $19.95   ISBN: 978-1-935387-92-3

To Order: 800-381-2700
Or, visit our website at www.hohmpress.com

Other HOHM PRESS Titles by Red Hawk

RETURN TO THE MOTHER
Poems of Self Remembering and Self Observation Inspired by Lao Tsu's Tao Te Ching
by Red Hawk

This collection of 94 contemporary poems brings the perennial wisdom of the *Tao Te Ching* into the twenty-first century—and adds the fragrance of Zen and Gurdjieff's dharma teachings in a spare poetic marriage with Lao Tsu.

The poet begs for a return to the true self, which he symbolizes as the place of the Mother within. This volume is a companion and completion to the author's trilogy, with his two previous volumes: *Self Observation* and *Self Remembering*.

Paper, 128 pages, $17.95   ISBN: 978-1-942493-30-3

Other Titles of Interest from HOHM PRESS

JUST THIS, 365
Wisdom and Wit from the Teachings of Lee Lozowick
by Lee Lozowick
compiled and edited by Regina Sara Ryan

This inspiring collection of short teachings are taken from the writings and personal communications of American spiritual teacher, Lee Lozowick (1943-2010).

Drawn from a wide variety of sources, including some of the author's never-before-published writings, *Just This 365* addresses such important topics as kindness, generosity and compassion; good humor and good company; self-observation; devotion and surrender to the Will of God; and presence and attention in everyday life and relationships.

Paper, 416 pages, $21.95   ISBN: 978-1-942493-29-7

Other Titles of Interest from HOHM PRESS

WINDS OF GRACE
Poetry, Stories and Teachings of Sufi Mystics and Saints
Renditions by Vraje Abramian

This book gathers together extracts from biographies of both Sufi and non-Sufi sages, stories and statements about them, as well as poetry attributed to them. The translator's intention is singular: to encourage individuals on their path. Reading works about and by saints and sages reminds us of the vital need in the wayfarer's life to keep focused on the Heart, the Divine, the Beloved, amidst so many contenders for one's attention.

Paperback with French flaps, 288 pages, $24.95
ISBN: 978-1-942493-06-8

• • •

KRISHNA'S HERETIC LOVERS
The Story of Chandidas & Rami ~ A Novel
by Mary Angelon Young

This novel of 14th-century Bengal recounts the passionate story of Chandidas, a young Brahmin priest, and Rami, a widow of low caste. This historical romance blends fiction and fact, love and sex, action and spiritual teachings, politics, and true characters with the authentic poetry written by the revered poet Chandidas (later known as the "Father of Bengali poetry").

Paper, 368 pages, $23.95   ISBN: 978-1-942493-19-8

To Order: 800-381-2700
Or, visit our website at www.hohmpress.com

Other Titles of Interest from HOHM PRESS

THE MIRROR OF THE SKY (book and CD)
Songs of the Bauls of Bengal
Translated by Deben Bhattacharya

Baul music today is prized by world musicologists, and Baul lyrics are treasured by readers of ecstatic and mystical poetry. Their music, lyrics and accompanying dance reflect the passion, the devotion and the iconoclastic freedom of this remarkable sect of musicians and lovers of the Divine, affectionately known as "God's troubadours."

The Mirror of the Sky is a translation of 204 songs, including an extensive introduction to the history and faith of the Bauls, and the composition of their music. It includes a CD of authentic Baul artists, recorded as much as forty years ago by Bhattacharya, a specialist in world music. The current CD is a rare presentation of this infrequently documented genre.

Paper, 288 pages, $24.95 (includes CD)
ISBN: 978-0-934252-89-8   CD sold separately, $16.95

• • •

THE WOMAN AWAKE
Feminine Wisdom for Spiritual Life
by Regina Sara Ryan

Through the stories and insights of great women whom the author has met or been guided by in her own journey, this book highlights many faces of the Divine Feminine: the silence, the solitude, the service, the power, the compassion, the art, the darkness, the sexuality. Read about: the Sufi poetess Rabia (8th century), contemporary Sufi master Irina Tweedie, Hildegard of Bingen, author Kathryn Hulme (*The Nun's Story*), German healer and mystic Dina Rees, and others. Includes personal interviews with contemplative Christian monk Tessa Bielecki, artist Meinrad Craighead and Zen roshi Joan Halifax.

Paper, 20+ photos, 518 pages, $19.95 ISBN: 978-0-934252-79-9

To Order: 800-381-2700
Or, visit our website at www.hohmpress.com

Other Titles of Interest from HOHM PRESS

NOBODY SON OF NOBODY
Poems of Shaikh Abu-Saeed Abil-Kheir
Renditions by Vraje Abramian

Anyone who has found a resonance with the love-intoxicated poetry of Rumi, must read the poetry of Shaikh Abil-Kheir. This renowned, but little-known Sufi mystic of the 10th century preceded Rumi by over two hundred years on the same path of annihilation into God. This book contains translations and poetic renderings of 195 short selections from the original Farsi, the language in which Abil-Kheir wrote.

These poems deal with the longing for union with God, the desire to know the Real from the false, the inexpressible beauty of creation when seen through the eyes of Love, and the many attitudes of heart, mind and feeling that are necessary to those who would find the Beloved, *The Friend*, in this life.

Paper, 104 pages, $12.95   ISBN: 978-1-890772-08-6

• • •

ENLIGHTENED DUALITY
Essays on Art, Beauty, Life and Reality As It Is
by Lee Lozowick and M. Young

This book of essays presents the essential teachings of the Western Baul spiritual master Lee Lozowick, with special emphasis on what he has named "Enlightened Duality." This dynamic spiritual principle suggests that one can combine a firmly-rooted and integrated awareness of the nondual ("all is One") nature of reality, with a lively, conscious relationship to the "duality" or play of opposites that characterizes our everyday lives. Unlike those strictly nondual perspectives that claim a "oneness" that relegates the human experience to an illusion of mind, Lozowick asserts that "unity is the law" and "Life is Real." Because this integration of spiritual principles into the whirl of daily relational life is often so challenging, a student's perspective is offered throughout the book, in commentaries by M. Young, a longtime apprentice of Lozowick's.

Paper, 608 pages, color and b&w photos, $24.95
ISBN: 978-1-935387-02-2

To Order: 800-381-2700
Or, visit our website at www.hohmpress.com

About the Author

Red Hawk was a Hodder Fellow at Princeton University, and currently teaches at the University of Arkansas at Monticello. His other books include: *Self Remembering: The Path to Non-Judgmental Love, A Practitioner's Manual* (Hohm Press, 2015); *Mother Guru: Savitri Love Poems* (Hohm Press, 2014); *Self Observation: The Awakening of Conscience: An Owner's Manual* (Hohm Press, 2009); *Raven's Paradise* (Bright Hill Press, 2010) winner 2008 Bright Hill Press poetry award, *Journey of the Medicine Man* (August House), *The Sioux Dog Dance* (Cleveland State University); *The Way of Power* (1996); *The Art of Dying* (1999); and *Wreckage with a Beating Heart* (Hohm Press, 2005). He has published in such magazines as *The Atlantic, Poetry,* and *Kenyon Review.* He has given readings with Allen Ginsberg (1994), Rita Dove (1995), Miller Williams (1996), Tess Gallagher (1996), and Coleman Barks (2005), and more than seventy solo-readings in the United States.

Red Hawk is available for readings, lectures and workshops. He may be contacted at 824 N. Hyatt, Monticello, Arkansas, 71655; or via e-mail at: moorer@uamont.edu

About Hohm Press

Hohm Press is committed to publishing books that provide readers with alternatives to the materialistic values of the current culture, and promote self-awareness, the recognition of interdependence, and compassion. Our subject areas include parenting, transpersonal psychology, religious studies, women's studies, the arts and poetry.

Contact Information: Hohm Press, PO Box 4410, Chino Valley, Arizona, 86323; USA; 800-381-2700, or 928-636-3331; email: hppublisher@cableone.net

Visit our website at www.hohmpress.com